Progressive Mental Toughness Training for Swimming:

Using Visualization to Reach Your True Potential

By

Joseph Correa

Certified Meditation Instructor

COPYRIGHT

ACKNOWLEDGEMENTS

To my family, who have stood behind me and believed in me no matter what.

CONTENTS

Progressive Mental Toughness Training for Swimming:

Using Visualization to Reach Your True Potential

By

Joseph Correa

Certified Meditation Instructor

INTRODUCTION

This book will significantly change how hard you can push yourself mentally and emotionally through visualization techniques taught in this book.

Want to be the best? To be the best you have to train physically and mentally to your maximum capacity. Visualizing is commonly thought of as an activity that cannot be quantified which makes it harder to see if you are improving or making a difference, but in reality visualizing will increase your chances of success much more than any other activity.

You will learn three visualization techniques that are proven to improve your performance under any situation. These are:

1. Motivational Visualization Techniques.
2. Problem Solving Visualization Techniques
3. Goal Oriented Visualization Techniques.

These swimming visualization techniques will help you:

- Win more often.
- Become mentally tougher.

- Outlast the competition.
- Get to the next level.
- Recover faster and train longer.

How is this possible? Visualizing will help you to better control your emotions, stress, anxiety, and performance under pressure situations that are often the difference between success and failure.

Bringing out the best in yourself in any sport and reaching your true potential can only happen through a balanced training regimen which should include: mental training, physical training, and proper nutrition.

Why aren't more people using visualizations to enhance their performance in swimming? There are a number of reasons but the truth is most people have never tried it before and are afraid to try something new. Others don't think that improving their mental capacity will make a difference but they are wrong.

Practicing visualization techniques for swimming on a regular basis will allow you to:

- Increase your lung capacity by helping you relax muscle tension and decrease workload.

- Recover faster after training or competing through breathing techniques that will reduce muscle stress.
- Overcome pressure situations.
- Train harder and longer without getting as tired.
- Reduce your chances of getting cramps and muscle tears.
- Improve control over your emotions under stressful conditions.
- See results you never thought possible.

Visualizing is hard work and requires constant practice which is why only the best do it and take all the glory. Be the best you can be by pushing yourself to your mental limit using visualizations.

ABOUT THE AUTHOR

As a certified meditation instructor, I am a strong believer in the power that can be harnessed from the mind and the regular practice of visualizations.

Having performed as a professional athlete, I understand what goes through your mind and how nerves and pressure can affect your performance.

The three biggest changes in my life have come from switching from a weight training approach to a more nutrition based, flexibility improved, and **mentally focused approach** which have had a significant change in my performance and in my life.

Visualizing has helped me control my emotions and thoughts by simulating live competitions before they even happened.

My knowledge and continued practice of visualizations has helped me live healthier and stronger throughout the years, which has benefitted me in all aspects of life. The more you use your brain to develop yourself and all that you can achieve, the more you will want to continue practicing visualizations.

Be dedicated and consistent with your visualization training sessions so that you too can see results that will blow your mind!

WHAT DOES IT MEAN TO VISUALIZE?

Visualizing is the practice of using your mind to imagine what you would like to see in your performance to improve it and reach new highs. When you are daydreaming you can't change your results but when you are visualizing you control every part of the imaging process so that you can recreate an exact scenario that you are confronted often with and learn to overcome it by seeing yourself do it over and over again.

Normally, you are going to be sitting or lying down. Close your eyes and then prepare yourself to get in the right mindset to create a mental movie where you decide what happens. You get to choose how you look, how you start, how you feel, and what the result will be. The goal is to positively change your mental habits by seeing them improve and develop to your favor as often as possible until they become your reality and can reach your maximum potential in live training or competition.

How you approach visualizing makes a big difference as it should be taken seriously and predetermined times should be set aside to preform your visualization sessions. These session can be used to work on specific things you feel you can improve on which can be: the outcome of your performance, your ability to control your nerves, your ability to control your emotions and prevent angry outbreaks, your capacity to adapt to changes in the environment, your thoughts, and your confidence level when performing.

Visualizations can have a powerful effect on your performance!

Visualizing requires a quiet environment and no interruptions so that you can focus to your best capacity and create the mental videos that you would like to see happen in real life which will better prepare your body to realize in a live situation.

Training your mind to imagine different scenarios and situations will give you more experience. When you can imagine more in depth and grow your capacity to focus and see things in more detail, you will have reached an ideal level of concentration in your visualization sessions which should be your goal.

WHY IS VISUALIZING IMPORTANT TO YOU?

Visualizing on a regular basis can have a very positive effect on your daily life but most importantly on your athletic performance. If you want to enhance your overall performance naturally and for the long term, visualizing is the way to go.

What does it mean to visualize?

Visualization techniques have been around for centuries but have not been used regularly in the athletic world until a couple of decades ago. Visualizations have not been as popular as certain other athletic training exercises such as: weight training, stretching, jump training, and other physical training methods.

Why is this? The answer to this question is simply that it hasn't been given as much attention because it's harder to grade, test or physically see results. Actual results are seen in your ability to push further and more confidently towards your goals, often reaching them more often than ever before.

Remember, your mind controls your body. The mind can be unlocked to have no limitations. If you think you're too small, too short, too slow, that's because you're measuring things on a physical plain. But what if I told you that a group of athletes are all physically the same and can jump as high and run as fast as the other will all have different results in the end? How can one person be superior to another? It would end up being who is mentally stronger and has a better capacity to overcome mental obstacles in any environment.

If everyone works just as hard and trains the same way, the mind will be the difference and visualizations will be the way to enhance your mental performance. **If this is the case, then visualization sessions will become the ultimate training tool to overcome the competition.**

Why is everyone working so hard to get stronger, faster, and more mobile? Simply, because they want to enhance their performance through what they think will give them the fastest and most effective results.

I completely agree with working hard physically and preparing the body for the grind and stress of

competition but just as in any sport or physical activity, the mind comes first.

Why does the mind come first? Mainly, because if you decide you can't do something before even starting then you simply won't achieve it no matter how many push-ups, sit-ups, squats, curls, sprints, or curls you do. Success can many times be decided as a possibility way before you even begin. If you decide you can achieve something your brain will work towards helping you achieve it no matter how many obstacles are in your way. If you do the opposite and decide you can't do it, then no matter how hard you try, it will always be much harder for you to be successful.

CHAPTER 1: VISUALIZING FOR ENHANCED PERFORMANCE IN SWIMMING

In recent years, athletes have come to realize that if you want to stay injury free and enhance your physical performance three things need to happen:

1. You have to become more flexible, agile, and mobile.
2. You need to recover better and faster after training and/or competing.
3. You need to prepare mentally for all types of internal and external conditions that might arise.

For the first, yoga and extended periods of stretching have become very popular and are now included in normal training regiments. This has reduced muscle tears and injuries that would normally come about if not done on a constant basis. Sport specific weight training and resistance training have become more common as athletes working to have an advantage over the competition.

The second has been improved though sports drinks, nutrient supplements, and better overall nutrition. Eating right and giving your body what it needs before and after training or competing is essential. This is one of the main reasons athletes can last much longer than years past which is also why many world records have been broken and top athletes have reached heights they never thought possible before. This is not the only reason but it's one of the main reasons performance has evolved for many athletes.

The third is the reason you are reading this book and the reason why you will change your future results. Mental toughness and emotional preparation will happen the fastest and will have the most powerful effects on your performance when you begin using visualization techniques as part of your training. It's not a secret any more that visualizations enhance performance to new levels but are not used as much as they will be in the future which is why you need to start right away to benefit from it before the rest do.

Many coaches and instructors require that their students do some form of yoga or stretching on a regular basis. In the future, I believe most coaches will require their students to do some form of visualizations or meditation on a daily or weekly basis.

How often should I visualize to see results?

How often you visualize depends on your capacity to concentrate and on your needs. If you are just starting with visualizations it would be best to start performing them on a day on and day off basis so you have a day break in between. For someone that feels they can visualize on a regular basis without losing focus can do it daily for 10 minutes to a half hour. Someone who has been visualizing regularly can visualize daily for an hour.

I would suggest you use the visualization techniques taught here on a daily basis at first to get good at it and then lower the sessions to organize them around a specific competition or training session so that you can maximize the effects of visualizing and enhance your performance for that specific moment.

Visualizations require practice to get better and develop your mental skills in ways that will unlock your abilities to see through the mind's eye or to simply imagine what you want to happen before it happens.

How will visualizations enhance my performance?

I have come to believe that athletes will reach their physical peak in most sports and athletic disciplines in the next decade because of advances in technology and in how athletes prepare for competition, which will bring everyone to search for a new competitive advantage or edge over the rest. This new edge will come from the mind and mainly though variations of visualization techniques and simulated scenarios where specific activities are performed mentally and then later physically. Too often athletes have no plan of action and simply learn from trial and error but by visualizing and developing simulated mental scenarios this will change how you prepare and ultimately how you perform.

Visualizing will enhance your performance in a number of ways. You will learn how to:

1. Control your muscular tension to relax more and save the real effort for that moment when you actually perform and not beforehand.

2. Control your heart rate to better control your emotions and nerves before, during and after competing or training to become efficient with your energy use.

3. Bring out your best performance under high pressure situations and unusual conditions that sometimes arise when you least expect them that end up making even the best athletes crumble when they normally outperform the rest.

4. Have a positive approach towards fear and nerves. Being able to find a way to overcome fear when you feel overwhelmed by the moment can be difficult but by rehearsing those moments mentally through your imagination you can prepare yourself to be in those moments and overcome them. Feeling nervous before competing is a natural reaction mainly to fear and the fear

of the unknown. When you visualize you can imagine moments in slow motion and think things through so that when you have to act in real time you don't feel pressured or rushed which are two of the main reasons most athletes end up underperforming.

5. Improve your ability to recover after competing or training by using breathing techniques and visualizations to relax the mind and creating a calm environment for your body to reduce the level of alertness it may be feeling due to nerves, adrenaline, stress, and emotional tension. This, by itself can be one of the greatest benefits for an athlete as being able to recover quickly and naturally can result in a long term increase in results. Some athletes have very short rest periods or days to recover in between competitions which is why being able to calm yourself down and recover faster is a big step forward mentally and physically.

6. Lower your level of anger towards others and yourself when under pressure or when you feel you are not performing the way you would want to. This can be frustrating but

learning to slow your breathing and to slow your thoughts down can allow you to respond in a positive and productive manner. Too many athletes become destructive when things don't go their way which only lowers all future potential to improve your capacities as an athlete. Using visualizations will help you to better control your emotions and erratic outbreaks that can cause you to underperform when there is no reason for them to exist when you are looking to do your very best.

7. Concentrate better and for longer periods of time. Not all athletic disciplines require long periods of concentration but even if you just need to focus for a short moment, this can be the difference between reaching new heights and taking a step back. Visualizing requires that you take the time to focus and imagine what you would like to happen in detail and for as long as necessary for you to create the environment you wish to see. This will become a valuable tool you will develop through the visualization techniques you will learn.

8. Feel more at peace with yourself. This might not be a priority for some but for others this could be what will help you to mature in your athletic life.

9. Increase your level of confidence on a daily basis by being prepared for all possible outcomes and visualizing the way you will react to them which in turn will guide you towards a path of success and away from failure. **Confidence is a difficult quality to develop and as it is the result of having success in a consistent manner but by seeing success in your mind as often as possible it will become part of your reality.** Make your visualization sessions a time to increase your confidence level in all aspects of your life.

10. Reduce distractions when performing or competing. Distractions can cause severe problems when trying to do your best. Learning not to look at unwanted places and people takes practice and discipline which can definitely be attained through visualizing.

CHAPTER 2: WHEN TO USE VISUALIZATIONS FOR SWIMMING

Visualizations should be used when you feel you have done your best physically and still don't find you have reached your athletic peak. For some athletes visualizing can be used for emotional purposes to better prepare for the stress of performing. For others it might be to reach a goal they have not reached yet. In either situation, visualizations should be used to enhance your performance and should be practiced in an organized and scheduled manner.

You can use visualizations when you wake up, during the day, or before going to sleep. This is more a matter of when you feel you will get the most out of it and will be the most productive time to stay still and focus on your mental images in a quiet and relaxed environment.

Before competitions or training sessions

For best results, visualizations should be used the day or night before a competition or practice session so that you can give your mind a chance to accept some of the thoughts you are trying to instill in it to get the results you want. For athletes who are practicing different visualization techniques or scenarios in training sessions in order to find what works best for them when it's time to compete, should use short visualization sessions of about 15 minutes the night before as to not interrupt sleep.

After competitions or training sessions

One of the greatest benefits of performing visualizations after competing or training is that you have instant feedback from actual results so you can instantly try to correct issues and solve problems with fresh imagery of what you were doing and what you need to be doing.

Information is fresh and images are sharp and easy to see even with your eyes closed when you have just competed. When visualizing, being able to see images and mental movies that you create in a detailed manner makes the moment feel more real and so will help you simulate the actual situation much closer to reality.

Definitely implement visualization sessions after competing and/or training to develop your potential and maximize a training session by using all your physical and mental strength.

Create a schedule for when to visualize

Make sure you take the time to plan a specific time and day or days of the week to perform your visualizations and decide what purpose they will have for that specific day. **It can be to help you focus on getting rid of nerves once per week, focusing on confidence building twice per week, and working on reaching your goals three days a week.** Decide for how long you are planning to visualize so that you don't rush or shorten your sessions due to other commitments.

Remember to plan for more time just in case you are interrupted on another day or are not able to finish a complete session on another specific day.

Results will come from persistence so don't try to do everything in one 5 or 6 hour session because that will not bring you long terms results. For long term results work to do 20-40 minutes sessions on a constant basis.

CHAPTER 3: THE BEST MEDITATION TECHNIQUES WHEN PREPARING TO VISUALIZE FOR SWIMMING

Why would you meditate to prepare to visualize?

To get the most out of visualizations you need to allow your mind and body to fully relax so that you can be more accepting and open to your potential. Meditating is simply using focused thoughts and combining them with breathing techniques to enhance your concentration towards what you want to achieve. For some athletes stretching or doing yoga after training or competing will get you ready to meditate and meditating will get you ready to visualize. That's the right process to prepare as an athlete to visualize and for this reason we will go over some brief meditation techniques you can use to prepare to visualize. These are great tools to learn and will become part of your routine if you want to get the most from your visualization sessions.

Mindfulness

During mindfulness, athletes should be trying to stay in the present in each and every thought that they currently have entering their mind.

This type of meditation teaches you to become aware of your breathing patterns, but doesn't attempt to change them in any way through breathing practices. This is a more passive form of meditation compared to other more active forms of meditation which will require you to change your breathing patterns. Mindfulness is one of the most common types of meditation in the world and one that all athletes can greatly benefit from.

Focused meditation

Athletes using meditation are directing their thoughts to a specific problem, emotion, or object they want to focus on and find a solution for.

Begin by clearing your mind of all distractions and then taking some time to focus on just a single sound, object, or thought. You are trying to focus for as long as possible in this state of mind where you can then redirect your concentration to an objective you want to achieve.

It's your choice if you want to move on to work on any other objective or thought, or you can also just maintain that initial focus on the sound, object, or thought you first had.

Movement meditation

Movement meditation is another form of meditation you should try as well. This is a type of meditation where you focus on your breathing patterns, moving the air into and out of your lungs, while doing flowing movement patterns (with your hands) which you will repeat. You might feel uncomfortable at the beginning by moving with your eyes closed but with time you will notice it is actually very relaxing and will help you to improve your overall health.

A mind to body connection will be optimized in this type of meditation, especially for people who have trouble staying still and prefer to move around in a natural flowing motion. These movements should be slow and repetitive. The more controlled they are, the better. Doing fast, or violent movements will undo the benefit of meditating.

People who practice yoga often find this form of meditation great as it is a good compliment and similar to yoga breathing and movement exercises. Both improve control over yourself and over thoughts. For people who have never done yoga before and have already done movement meditation, will find that warming up with some yoga based exercises can often help you ease into movement meditation faster. The goal is to enter a meditative state quicker and yoga will definitely allow you to do this in a natural way. While yoga focuses more on improving flexibility and developing muscle strength, movement meditation is directed more towards a mental state and slow breathing patterns.

CHAPTER 4: PREPARING YOURSELF TO VISUALIZE BY CREATING THE RIGHT ENVIRONMENT

After you decide what type of meditation technique you will be using to prepare to visualize, you need to prepare the area around you so that you have the right environment to visualize in.

EQUIPMENT: Place a mat, blanket, towel, or chair where you plan to visualize.

Some people prefer to use a towel (which is great when you are traveling or out of town), or a mat to sit on or lay flat on your back on. Others prefer to sit on a chair to have a stable position that will help you not to fall asleep if you feel too relaxed.

I prefer to sit on a yoga mat as it is a position that I feel helps me focus and relax. Sometimes I warm up with yoga or static stretching so I will already have my mat ready but when I travel I simply use a thick towel.

Being comfortable is very important to get in the right state of mind so make sure you use the right equipment to get started.

TIME: Decide how long you will visualize for in advance

Make sure you decide beforehand for how long you plan on visualizing and with what purpose. For something simple like focusing on being positive and breathing, you can plan on doing a short session of about 5 to 15 minutes long. Whereas if you plan on focusing on a problem and want to try and find a solution for, you might want to plan on giving yourself enough time to first relax through breathing patterns and then start to focus on alternative solutions to the problem at hand. This might take anywhere from 10 minutes to an hour or longer depending on your level of experience in meditating or it may also depend on how long it takes you to get in a relaxed state of mind that will allow you to focus well enough to confront the problem.

Plan on how long you will take so that you can prepare beforehand to stay at the same location until you're done without interruptions such as:

being hungry, kids coming into the room, bathroom breaks, etc. Take care of these possible distractions beforehand.

LOCATION: Finding a clean, quiet, and comfortable space to visualize

Find a place where you can totally relax and clear your mind with no interruptions. This can be anywhere you feel comfortable and can reach this relaxed state of mind. It could be on the grass in a park, at home in your room, in your bathroom, in a quiet empty room, or by yourself in your car. This is completely up to you. Make sure you don't choose a location where you may have work close to you or a cell phone that keeps ringing or vibrating. TURN YOUR CELL PHONE OFF! It's impossible to get the results you want from meditating by having constant distractions and now a days cell phones are a main source of distraction and interruptions.

PREPARATION: Prepare your body to visualize

Before visualizing make sure you do whatever you need to do to get your body relaxed and ready. This could be by taking a shower, stretching, putting on comfortable clothes, etc.

Make sure you eat or drink a nutritious shake at least 30 minutes before starting so that you don't feel hungry or too full. A lean meal would be ideal to help you prepare properly beforehand. I will go into more depth on the importance of nutrition in one of the following chapters.

WARM UP: Do some Yoga or stretch beforehand to start relaxing.

For some of you who have already done yoga in the past, know how relaxing it can be. Those of you who have not started doing yoga, it would be a good time to start since it will help you to better relax and calm yourself down. It's not necessary to do yoga before meditating but it helps in order to maximize the effects and speed up the relaxing process to get you in the right state of mind. Stretching is another good alternative since stretching combined with some breathing exercises will help you calm down and feel more at ease.

MENTALITY: Do some deep breathing to start calming yourself down

Breathing is easy but practicing breathing takes more time. The benefits of practicing breathing techniques are many.

Most athletes will find themselves recovering faster after intense moments. They will also notice they are able to stay focused even when out of breath. ATHLETES NEED TO LEARN TO BREATHE! Athletes need to focus on the air moving into and out of their lungs, pay attention to how the body expands and contracts. Hearing and feeling the air move in and out of your nose and mouth will help you feel more relaxed and is the proper to focus on your breathing. Every time you breathe in and is then exhaled try to focus on going into a deeper and deeper state of relaxation. Every time oxygen fills your lungs your body will feel more energized and full of positive emotions.

ENVIRONMENT: Add some calm and relaxing music in the background only if it does not become a distraction.

If music helps you get into a relaxed state, by all means include it in your visualization session. Everything and anything that helps you get into a more focused and relaxed state should be used, including music.

If you feel you are able to clear your mind better without any sounds or music, then don't add music to your environment.

I normally don't add music simply because I find music takes me in other directions which I don't always want to go since some music reminds me of other thoughts and ideas. That's just me but maybe music is right for you. Try both options to see what works better for you. Some athletes like to listen to music before competing since they feel it relaxes them or gets them in the right mood. Find what works for you and stick to it.

VISUALIZATION POSITIONS

When it comes to visualization positions it's basically up to you. There is no wrong or right position, only the one that gets you in the best state of concentration. For some people sitting on a chair is great because of the back support, while others prefer to be closer to the ground and will decide to sit on a towel.

Sitting position

For the sitting position simply find a chair that you feel will allow you to focus without making you feel too uncomfortable or that relaxes you too much where you feel sleepy. Make sure your back is straight when seated and that your feet can touch the floor as you don't want to finish your visualization session with back pain. Some people prefer to add a soft pillow to their chair to feel more comfortable.

Kneeling on the floor

Take your shoes and socks off if you want to and kneel on the ground. Try kneeling on top of a soft mat or folded towel as to have your toes pointing behind you and your hips directly above your heels.

Your back should be straight and relaxed as to allow your lungs to expand and contract as much times as necessary. You want to create a strong connection through your breathing and to do this, air has to go in and out of your lungs in a flowing motion.

Laying down position

Lay down on the mat, towel, or blanket and relax your feet and hands. Your hands should stay at your sides and your feet pointing up or outwards. Your hands can be placed on your stomach in a gentle but still position or at your sides. Your head needs to stay facing the ceiling or the sky. If you tilt it to one side or another, this will not allow you to stay focused for long periods of time and might even end up with some neck tension. This is a great position to visualize in (when done correctly) as long as you don't fall asleep. If this is your problem, simply choose another position.

Butterfly position

In this position you will need to sit down on your mat or towel, open your legs and then bring your feet together so that the bottom of each is facing one another. Your knees might flare upwards or they might be able to go down to the ground, it does not matter as long as you feel comfortable and can relax in this position. Make sure your spine is straight and balanced.

CHAPTER 5: BREATHING TECHNIQUES TO MAXIMIZE YOUR VISUALIZATION EXPERIENCE AND ENHANCE YOUR PERFORMANCE

Breathing patterns will be the key to set the pace of your visualization session and also to get into a hyper focused state.

When visualizing, you want to pay attention to breathing patterns and direct them through your session. All breathing patterns should be done by breathing in through your nose and out through your mouth.

In order to get into a more relaxed state, your heart rate needs to drop and to do this, breathing will be essential. The patterns you use will facilitate this process to help you reach higher levels of concentration. With practice these breathing patterns will become second nature to you. Decide beforehand if slow breathing patterns are better for you or if fast breathing patterns will be what you need. Slow breathing patterns relax you and fast breathing patterns energize you.

SLOW BREATHING PATTERNS

In order to slow down your breathing you will want to take in air slowly and for a longer period of time and then release it slowly as well. For athletes, this type of breathing is good to get you to relax after training or about an hour before competition. Different ratios of air in and air out will affect your level of relaxation, and in turn your ability to reach an optimal level of visualization.

Normal slow breathing pattern: Start by taking air in through your nose slowly and counting to 5. Then, release slowly counting back down from 5 to 1. You should repeat this process 4 to 10 times until you feel completely relaxed and ready to focus. Athletes should focus on breathing in through the nose and out through the mouth for this type of breathing pattern.

Extended slow breathing pattern: Start by taking air in through your nose slowly and counting to 7. Then, release slowly counting back down from 7 to 1 while exhaling out through your mouth. You should repeat this process 4 to 6 times until you feel completely relaxed and ready to focus.

Slow breathing pattern for hyperactive athletes:
Start by taking air in through your nose slowly and counting to 3. Then, release slowly counting back down from 6 to 1 while exhaling out through your mouth. You should repeat this process 4 to 6 times until you feel relaxed and ready to focus. This pattern will force you to slow down completely. The last repetition of this sequence should end with 4 seconds in and 4 seconds out to stabilize your breathing.

Ultra slow breathing pattern: Begin by taking air in through your nose slowly and counting to 4. Then, release slowly counting back down from 10 to 1 while exhaling out through your mouth. You should repeat this process 4 to 6 times until you feel completely relaxed and ready to visualize. This pattern will force you to slow down gradually. The last 2 repetitions of this sequence should end with 4 seconds in and 4 seconds out to stabilize your breathing and balance the air in and out ratio.

Stabilizing breathing patterns before meditating:
This is a good type of breathing pattern that should be used if you feel you are already calm and want to start immediately meditating. Start by taking air

in through your nose slowly and counting to 3. Then, release slowly counting back down from 3 to 1. You should repeat this process 7 to 10 times until you feel completely relaxed and ready to focus. Athletes should focus on breathing in through the nose and out through the mouth for this type of breathing pattern.

FAST BREATHING PATTERNS

Fast breathing patterns are very important for athletes in order to get energized and ready to compete. Even though this type of breathing pattern is most effective when visualizing, it will be just as useful for meditating. For athletes that are very calm and need to feel more in control of their mind might want to use these patterns to get themselves ready to visualize.

Normal fast breathing pattern: Start by taking air in through your nose slowly and counting to 5. Then, release slowly counting back down from 3 to 1. You should repeat this process 6 to 10 times until you feel completely relaxed and ready to visualize. Athletes should focus on breathing in through the nose and out through the mouth for this type of breathing pattern.

Prolonged fast breathing pattern: Start by taking air in through your nose slowly and counting to 10. Then, release slowly counting back down from 5 to 1 while exhaling out through your mouth. You should repeat this process 5 to 6 times until you feel completely relaxed. If you have trouble getting to 10 at first, simply lower the count to 7 or 8. Focus on breathing in through the nose and out through the mouth.

Pre-competition fast breathing pattern: Start by taking air in through your nose slowly and counting to 6. Then, release quickly in one breath while exhaling out through your mouth. You should repeat this process 5 to 6 times until you feel completely relaxed and ready to focus. You can add 2 repetitions to this sequence with 4 seconds in and 4 seconds out to stabilize your breathing and balance the air in and out ratio.

All of these types of breathing patterns are performance enhancing and can be used during competition depending on your level of energy or nervousness.

For athletes that get nervous before competition you should use slow breathing patterns.

For athletes that need to get energized before competition you should use the fast breathing patterns.

In case of anxiety, a combination of slow breathing patterns followed by fast breathing patterns will give you optimal results.

During training sessions or during competition when feeling exhausted or out of breath use the normal fast breath breathing pattern to help recover quicker.

Breathing patterns are a great way to control your levels of intensity which in turn will save you energy and allow you to recover faster.

CHAPTER 6: PROPER NUTRITION TO MAXIMIZE YOUR VISUALIZATION RESULTS IN SWIMMING

Why is nutrition important when you are planning to visualize?

To maximize the effects of visualizing it's important to have a balanced diet through meals and/or juices or shakes. Improving your physical condition will require that you strengthen your mental toughness and you're eating habits so that you have enough energy for prolonged visualization sessions specially after training or competing. When you visualize you need to stay focused for a minimum period of time that can become longer if you feel you need more time. When you are staying still and focused for longer periods of time you need to make sure your body is well nourished and make sure it will not become a distraction by being hungry or too full which can be an important issue to take care of beforehand. If you eat something that gives you stomach problems stay away from it before starting your visualization session.

What should I eat or drink before visualizing?

The ideal pre-visualization foods you should consume are: Lean proteins, omega fats, vegetables and legumes, and water are and should be eaten in appropriate amounts depending on your caloric needs.

To help you prepare to visualize I am including some high nutrient and high protein shakes and/or juices to make your digestive process less of a distraction while you are visualizing and to have the most amount of energy before beginning.

Drinking these shakes 30-60 minutes before visualizing will give you the best results and will keep you from feeling hungry or too full to completely relax and concentrate on the session your about to perform.

If you don't have time eat right make sure you at least drink something that will nourish your body and not just make you feel full as you need to focus on quality not quality when it comes to what you eat and drink.

Protein

Lean proteins are very important to develop and repair muscle tissue. Lean proteins also help to normalize hormone concentrations in the body which will allow you to control your mood as well as your temper. Some of the best lean proteins you can have are:

- Turkey breast (all natural if possible).
- Lean red meat (all natural as well).
- Egg whites
- Most dairy products.
- Chicken breast (All natural).
- Quinoa
- Nuts (all varieties)

Omega fats

Omega fats are easy to obtain and very important for your body functions, especially for the brain. Omega fats are commonly found in:

- Salmon (Preferably wild, non-farmed)
- Walnuts (An easy to carry around snack)
- Flaxseeds (Blend them with any shake)

- Sardines

You will notice your brain functions improve and your brains' overall health increase. Your immune system should also get stronger which will reduce your chances of getting cancer, diabetes, and other serious health related problems.

Vegetables and Legumes

Vegetables and legumes are not given enough importance. Find a vegetable you enjoy eating and include it in your diet. It will pay off as the years go by. When you hear people talking about how important it is to have a balanced diet, they are also referring to vegetables. Some of the best vegetables and legumes to include in your daily meals are:

- Tomatoes
- Carrots
- Beets
- Kale
- Spinach
- Cabbage
- Parsley

- Broccoli
- Brussel sprouts
- Lettuce
- Radish
- Green, red, and yellow peppers
- Cucumber
- Egg plant
- Avocado

You want to make sure you get a wide variety of colors to make sure you get different vitamins and minerals.

Fruits

Fruits also contain a large amount of vitamins necessary for your body to perform to its maximum capacity. Antioxidants help your body to recover faster which is extremely important for athletes. Make sure you eat many fruits that are high on antioxidants after training or competing. Fruits provide an important source of dietary fiber which allows you to process food easier. Some of the best fruits to include in your pre-mediation diet are:

- Apples (green and red)

- Oranges
- Grapes (red and green)
- Bananas
- Grapefruit (A bit sour but full of antioxidants)
- Lemons and limes (In the form of juice mixed with water. I often ask for water and some slices of lemon when I go out to eat as these are wonderful antioxidants as well).
- Cherries (natural, not the sugar coated).
- Mandarins
- Watermelon
- Cantaloupe

Water

Water and hydration are very important in your body's development and can increase the amount of energy you have during the day. Drinking juices and shakes will help but are not substitutes to drinking water. The amount of water you drink will depend on the amount of cardiovascular training you do, this might be more than the usual suggested. Most people should drink at least 8 glasses of water a day but most athletes should drink 10 -14 glasses of water.

Ever since I started to carry around my gallon of water I am able to reach my "1 gallon a day" goal of water which has improved my health significantly.

Some of the benefits I have noticed and most people will notice are:

- Less or no headaches (Brain is hydrated more often)
- Improved digestion.
- Less tired during the day.
- More energy in the morning.
- Reduced amount of visible wrinkles.

- Less cramps or signs of muscle tightness. (This is a common problem for many athletes.)
- Better concentration (this will benefit you a lot when meditating).
- Decreased desire for sweets and snacks in between meals.

SAMPLE SHAKE RECIPES FOR

PRE-VISUALIZATION SESSIONS

Here are some examples of high protein shake recipes for athletes you can add to your pre-visualization diet. If you want to modify some of the ingredients or the quantities feel free to do so.

IF VISUALIZING AFTER BREAKFAST

Super Mix Shake

Depending on your metabolism, you will adapt to some of the shakes better than others. For those of you who prefer a sweeter flavor in your shakes, this is a good choice. You can adapt certain ingredients to change the flavor to your preference like the caramel, hazelnuts, or vanilla yogurt.

Preparation:

Mix all the ingredients together in a juicer or blender at high speed and then enjoy a delicious shake.

Ingredients:

- 12 oz. fat-free milk

- 2 tbsp. fat free vanilla yogurt or Kefir

- 1 tbsp. reduced fat peanut butter

- 2 tbsp. spoon hazelnuts

- 1 tbsp. caramel ice cream topping

Nutritional Facts:

- Calories: 430

- Proteins: 23g

- Carbs: 20g

- Fat: 11g

Lean mass Banana Shake

People who stick to a muscle gain diet or routine will benefit even more if they add muscle shakes because of the ease of preparation and because of how fast the body can absorb the protein and nutrients.

Preparation:

Mix all the ingredients together in a juicer or blender at high speed and then enjoy a delicious shake.

Ingredients:

- 1/2 frozen banana

- 2 tbsp. Whipping cream (heavy cream, not cream out of a can)

- 2 eggs

- 10-12 oz. water

Nutritional Facts:

- Calories: 320

- Proteins: 18g

- Carbs: 15g

- Fat: 9g

Sweet Boost Shake

Here is a great example of a shake recipe that has very different ingredients, but combined they are a great source of protein and will increase your gym performance.

Preparation:

Mix all the ingredients together in a juicer or blender at high speed and then enjoy a delicious shake.

Ingredients:

- 1 medium to large banana

- 8 oz. light Milk

- 1 tbsp. Flaxseed and Almond Mixture

- 1 tsp Maple Syrup

- Few drops of vanilla essence/extract

- 1 tbsp. low-fat natural yogurt

Nutritional Facts:

- Calories: 450

- Proteins: 19g

- Carbs: 16g

- Fat: 10g

Orange Shake

Let's start the day with an awesome shake to boost our immune system and help you increase more muscle. This recipe is high in vitamin C and potassium because of the strawberries and orange juice which will also allow your muscles to recover faster.

Preparation:

Mix all the ingredients together in a juicer or blender at high speed and then enjoy a delicious shake.

Ingredients:

- 8 oz. Orange Juice

- 1 tsp. Vanilla Extract

- ½ banana

- 2-3 frozen strawberries

- 2 tsp. honey

Nutritional Facts:

- Calories: 291

- Proteins: 15g

- Carbs: 12g

- Fat: 5g

Almond Shake Blast

Plan on having a better digestion after having this shake with this combination of oatmeal, raisins, almonds, and peanut butter. The raisins give it a great flavor and the oatmeal gives it a different texture than other shakes.

Preparation:

Mix all the ingredients together in a juicer or blender at high speed and then enjoy a delicious shake.

Ingredients:

- 10-12 oz. of skim milk

- 1.2 cup of raw oatmeal

- 1.2 cup of raisins

- 12 shredded almonds

- 1 tbsp. of peanut butter.

Nutritional Facts:

- Calories: 380

- Proteins: 18g

- Carbs: 15g

- Fat: 12g

Wild berry Shake

Raspberries are known to be very high on vitamin C and antioxidants which many medical professionals suggest as an anti-cancer supplement to your normal day to day foods and meals. You can replace an ordinary snack with this healthy drink that is not very high on protein but will help take a break from all the other high protein shakes you will be taking on a daily basis.

Preparation:

Mix all the ingredients together in a juicer or blender at high speed and then enjoy a delicious shake.

Ingredients:

- 8 raspberries

- 4 strawberries

- 15 blueberries

- 16 ounces non-fat milk

Nutritional Facts:

- Calories: 210

- Proteins: 9g

- Carbs: 10g

- Fat: 8g

Peanut Banana Shake

In terms of nutrition this shake is high on lean protein and complex carbs, so it will increase muscle growth and recovery. It will also give you an energy boost while you're training if you drink it half hour before.

Preparation:

Mix all the ingredients together in a juicer or blender at high speed and then enjoy a delicious shake.

Ingredients:

- ½ cup Peanuts

- 1/2 Banana

- 1 Cup Skim Milk

- 1/4 Cup Quaker Oats

- Pinch of Salt

Nutritional Facts:

- Calories: 230

- Proteins: 18g

- Carbs: 12g

- Fat: 5g

Carrot Pineapple Shake

This shake might look a little strange for you guys, but believe me it's a good one for you and your body. You can remove or lower the portions for some of the ingredients depending on your preference as this mix is very different from some of the others.

Preparation:

Mix all the ingredients together in a juicer or blender at high speed and then enjoy a delicious shake.

Ingredients:

- 1 cup chocolate milk

- 3/4 c shredded carrots

- 10 frozen pineapple chunks

- 2 tsp unsweetened shredded coconut

- 1 tsp vanilla

Nutritional Facts:

- Calories: 220

- Proteins: 21g

- Carbs: 13g

- Fat: 13g

Blueberry Apple Shake

Maintaining a high level of energy is the goal of this shake. It will also provide you with some lean proteins that will help you even if you're a bit tired that day or if you just want to push yourself harder that day.

Preparation:

Mix all the ingredients together in a juicer or blender at high speed and then enjoy a delicious shake.

Ingredients:

- 1/2 small apple cut into small pieces (with skin)
- 1/2 cup cherries (dark, sweet, pitted)
- 1/2 cup blueberries
- 1/2 cup whey or milk protein

Nutritional Facts:

- Calories:300
- Proteins: 39g
- Carbs: 18g
- Fat: 5g

Cherry Banana Shake

Two great tasting ingredients in one shake to give you lots of energy. Cherries and bananas are provide a great source of fiber that your body needs when taking in large portions of protein. Try this drink before any training session night or day.

Preparation:

Mix all the ingredients together in a juicer or blender at high speed and then enjoy a delicious shake.

Ingredients:

- 1/2 cup cherries (dark, sweet, pitted)
- 1/2 cup Banana
- 1/2 cup whey or milk protein

Nutritional Facts:

- Calories:300
- Proteins: 39g
- Carbs: 18g
- Fat: 5g

Egg Mania Shake

The chick peas give it a green color but don't really change the flavor at all. This is a great combination of proteins and carbs.

Preparation:

Mix all the ingredients together in a juicer or blender at high speed and then enjoy a delicious shake.

Ingredients:

- 4 egg whites

- 1 banana

- 1/4 cup chick peas

- pineapple slices

- Coconut milk

- Coconut extract can be added

Nutritional Facts:

- Calories:280

- Proteins: 25g

- Carbs: 40g

- Fat: 4g

High Protein Honey Shake

Increase your gym performance by increase the amounts of protein you have on a daily basis. This shake is high on protein and high on flavor.

Preparation:

Mix all the ingredients together in a juicer or blender at high speed and then enjoy a delicious shake.

Ingredients:

- 1/2 c water

- 1 scoop Whey or milk Protein Powder

- 2 tbsp. Honey

- 1 tbsp. Smooth Peanut Butter

Nutritional Facts:

- Calories:114

- Proteins: 34g

- Carbs: 5.2g

- Fat: 4.5g

Fruit Mix Shake

This shake recipe can easily replace your breakfast but this still have a healthy portion of food to nourish your body. It has a lot of the nutrients your body needs to have a good start in the morning. Protein and carbs are included in this recipe to give your energy and strength when training.

Preparation:

Mix all the ingredients together in a juicer or blender at high speed and then enjoy a delicious shake.

Ingredients:

- 1/2 cup of chopped strawberries

- 1 small apple

- 1 small plum

- 1 cup of chocolate milk

- 1 tbsp. of smooth peanut butter

Nutritional Facts:

- Calories:700

- Proteins: 46g

- Carbs: 90g

- Fat: 20g

Choco Shake

A great way of combining a dark chocolate bar with the right ingredients to obtain a shake that will increase your gym performance and muscle gain.

Preparation:

Mix all the ingredients together in a juicer or blender at high speed and then enjoy a delicious shake.

Ingredients:

- 1 dark chocolate bar

- 4 eggs

- 3 cups milk

- 1 scoop Whey Protein Powder

Nutritional Facts:

- Calories: 290

- Proteins: 45g

- Carbs: 37g

- Fat: 19g

-

Taste of Everything Shake

This shake recipe is an excellent source of fiber your body needs. It's full of nutrients and vitamins that will you both more energy and more vitality.

Preparation:

Mix all the ingredients together in a juicer or blender at high speed and then enjoy a delicious shake.

Ingredients:

- Grapes, 4 grapes, seedless
- Blackberries, fresh, 0.5 grams
- Blueberries, fresh, 25 berries
- Strawberries, fresh, 0.5 grams
- Pineapple, fresh, 1 slice, thin (3-1/2" diameter x 1/2" thick
- Apples, fresh, 10 grams
- Yogurt, plain, low fat, 0.5 container (4 oz.)
- Kale, 0.5 grams
- Oranges, 0.5 grams

Nutritional Facts:

- Calories: 280

- Proteins: 48g

- Carbs: 31g

- Fat: 4.2g

Wake up Now Shake

Here is how you should start the day, energy will be the defining word for this shake, but don't think it's not good for gaining muscle too, because you would be wrong.

Preparation:

Mix all the ingredients together in a juicer or blender at high speed and then enjoy a delicious shake.

Ingredients:

- 1 fresh banana, medium

- 2 servings (60 grs) oat flakes

- 1-2 tbsp. peanut butter, smooth style

- 1 cup (250 ml) yogurt, plain, low fat (0% - 1.5% mf)

- 0.5 tbsp. (or less) cinnamon, ground

Nutritional Facts:

- Calories:650

- Proteins: 28g

- Carbs: 85g

- Fat: 10g

Mango Tango Shake

This is a great shake you can add to other days so you can take two shakes per day since it is high on fiber and low on fat. This lean shake will help you fight any tiredness in the gym and will improve your performance.

Preparation:

Mix all the ingredients together in a juicer or blender at high speed and then enjoy a delicious shake.

Ingredients:

- 2 large strawberries, fresh or frozen

- 1 cup Orange Juice

- 1/2 mango, fresh or frozen

- 1 scoop Milk Protein Powder

Nutritional Facts:

- Calories:250

- Proteins: 30.5g

- Carbs: 52g

- Fat: 8.4g

Pineapple Tangerine Shake

To gain muscle, there is no secret; you have to train and eat right! You will struggle if you don't have enough energy while training and that's why adding ingredients that will give you a boost when necessary will make all the difference when trying to build stronger muscles.

Preparation:

Mix all the ingredients together in a juicer or blender at high speed and then enjoy a delicious shake.

Ingredients:

- 1/2 cup Pineapple, frozen chunks

- 1/2 cup Tangerines, (mandarin oranges), canned

- 2 tsp. honey

- 1 scoop Whey Protein Powder

Nutritional Facts:

- Calories:150

- Proteins: 39g

- Carbs: 17g

- Fat: 11g

Peanut Butter Apple Shake

Shakes can be a great source of calories and energy which are necessary to increase muscle mass. This delicious shake recipe is made to help you increase your muscle gain and maintain a high level of energy.

Preparation:

Mix all the ingredients together in a juicer or blender at high speed and then enjoy a delicious shake.

Ingredients:

- 3/4 Cup plain or vanilla yogurt

- 2 tbsp. Peanut Butter

- 1 Banana

- 1/8 Cup milk

- 3/4 Cup ice

- 1 apple

   Nutritional Facts:

- Calories:440

- Proteins: 22g

- Carbs: 50g

- Fat: 19g

Banana Super Shake

Vanilla almond milk will make this a great protein shake. It promotes muscle mass growth without unbalancing your diet. You can reduce or eliminate the cinnamon to make it to your specific preference.

Preparation:

Mix all the ingredients together in a juicer or blender at high speed and then enjoy a delicious shake.

Ingredients:

- 1/2 cup vanilla almond milk
- 1/2 cup water
- 1/2 banana
- Dash of cinnamon
- 1 scoop of vanilla protein powder

Nutritional Facts:

- Calories:350
- Proteins: 43g
- Carbs: 25g
- Fat: 5g

Dark Oat Power Shake

The combination of dark chocolate, cottage cheese, and oatmeal will increase your muscle development, and get you that energy boost that you were looking for in the gym while improve digestion and strengthening your heart.

Preparation:

Mix all the ingredients together in a juicer or blender at high speed and then enjoy a delicious shake.

Ingredients:

- 1/2 cup of Cottage Cheese (or 1 cup Greek yoghurt)

- 1/2 - 1 cup water (depending on desired thickness) or milk

- 10g dark chocolate

- ½ cup raw oatmeal

- 1/2 banana

Nutritional Facts:

- Calories:150

- Proteins: 40g

- Carbs: 20g

- Fat: 8g

Milk Protein Shake

To build and maintain your muscles you need to increase carbohydrates and protein so that you have the energy to work hard and the ingredients to allow your muscles to fully develop.

Preparation:

Mix all the ingredients together in a juicer or blender at high speed and then enjoy a delicious shake.

Ingredients:

- 1 scoop Milk protein powder

- 1/2 bananas

- 1/2 cup almond slices

- 8 oz milk

- 3 ice cubes

Nutritional Facts:

- Calories:335

- Proteins: 31g

- Carbs: 25g

- Fat: 18g

Avocado Shake

Protein shakes with vegetables are uncommon but should be more normal because of the value they bring to your diet and to your body. Avocado is considered by some as a "super food" and is great for your body.

Preparation:

Mix all the ingredients together in a juicer or blender at high speed and then enjoy a delicious shake.

Ingredients:

- 1/2 avocado

- 1 tbsp. shredded coconut

- 1 cup almond milk

- 1 scoop Whey Protein Powder

Nutritional Facts:

- Calories:300

- Proteins: 35g

- Carbs: 20g

- Fat: 8g

CHAPTER 7: VISUALIZATION TECHNIQUES FOR IMPROVED SWIMMING RESULTS

Is there a wrong or right way to visualize?

There is no wrong or right way of visualizing. You need to search for the right fit for you. Create the right environment to visualize in and allow your mind to amplify the possibilities through proper techniques. Make sure you find a comfortable place to start at. Either sit or rest on a comfortable chair, mat, or towel much like you do when you meditate.

When you visualize you are taking meditation to the next level and want to use much of the same process you do for meditating.

The three main types of visualization techniques:

There are many types of visualizations that can be performed. Three common types are motivational visualizations, problem solving visualizations, and goal oriented visualizations.

Athletes in all fields commonly use visualizations in one form or another sometimes without even knowing they are doing them. For some, it's done while being awake which is what is known as day dreaming and for others this might happen in their dreams but with no control over the outcome.

When you are visualizing you are in control of everything you're seeing in your mind and can design the beginning and ending however you like. Being creative is useful since things don't always come out the way we plan them to in real life but by preparing mentally and emotionally for all possible outcomes, things become easier to handle when it comes time to perform. Peak performance is a term used for when you are "in the zone" and at your very best. It is easier to perform at your peak when you have prepared your mind through visualizations.

Why visualize to motivate yourself?

Some people have trouble finding the right motivation under pressure to do what they are supposed to be doing instead of being intimidated by their surroundings and people watching them. By motivating yourself through visualizations and by telling yourself to do better and push yourself harder as you see the thoughts you want to realize in your mind, you will unlock the brains possibilities to get you through the fear, anxiety, nervousness, and pressure involved when competing.

What are problem solving visualizations?

Problem solving visualizations are a common form of mental training and can be the most useful of all visualization techniques. Often, athletes find they keep making the same mistakes over and over only to find the same result. This is because they need to take the time to analyze the situation and search for all possible solutions to their problems. Simply finding time to visualize will be time well spent when you need to solve a specific problem. Having too many distractions during the day, both mental and visual, can slow down the speed at which you could find a solution to what you would like to correct. It could be a habit you have formed that you can't get rid of. It can also be that you do your worst right when it counts the most. Other times it can be that you lose your temper or get too emotional right when you need to keep your cool.

There are many possible situations an athlete can be in and not know how to approach them is the main reason success is delayed or never realized.

The first step is to find the time to problem solve and visualize.

The second step to problem solving is to determine what the problem is and how it's affecting you.

The third step is to find alternative solutions that can take you in the right direction or that can eliminate the problem. In some cases, you might have to ask others who have been in similar situations and find out how they approached this problem and if their solution is an option for you.

The fourth step is to visualize how you would physically perform this solution and make it as vivid and real as you can.

The fifth step is to make corrections when you have mentally seen that it won't work and find an alternative. You can also simply apply the solution in real life and if it does not work go back to visualizing later to find a better solution. This is more of a "trial and error" method than visualization technique but can be used as a practical tool to get you there by combining it with visualizations.

What are goal oriented visualizations?

Goal oriented visualizations are mental images and videos you want to create in your brain when visualizing that focus on achieving a specific objective. This may be: winning a competition, improving your record time, training more hours a day, adding "X" amount of protein to your diet, not getting tired as much (some of these are results based goals and some are performance based goals. Both are important when planning your visualization session and future progress as an athlete.)

This is what you train physically for. To see results at the end of all the hard work. Using visualizations completes the training by doing the last and most important part of preparing for competition. You prepare your mind and body to perform at their best so that you can do it when it counts the most. Nutrition and physical training will prepare your body. Meditation, breathing patterns, and visualizations will prepare your brain. The combination of both will give you the greatest competitive advantage and that's you want.

CHAPTER 8: VISUALIZATION TECHNIQUES: MOTIVATIONAL VISUALIZATIONS

Learning to get inspired

Getting inspired by seeing yourself be successful through visualizations is a great image to experience and a wonderful effect visualizing can create in your life. Learn to get inspired and believe things are possible in your own life because they are. Athletes often limit themselves because they don't dream big enough. With a little planning and some discipline many things are possible no matter how difficult they may seem.

What are motivational visualizations?

Motivational visualizations are mental images you will create where you see yourself being confident, radiant, and successful. Inspiring yourself through an amplified positive self-image is powerful and can have ripple effects in other parts of your life.

You should be imagining yourself reach a goal when visualizing.

These are some questions you want to ask yourself when preparing to perform motivational visualizations:

- How would you like to dress to compete if you could choose any uniform, clothes, or attire?
- How would you walk before competing if you had all the confidence in the world?
- What would be the perfect environment for you to compete in?
- What facial expressions would you have if you were to win?
- How would you look if you lost 10 pounds of fat and were leaner, faster, and more explosive?
- How would you look if you felt confident?
- What would you do if you won the competition or reached your goal?

By seeing yourself being successful with a goal you are trying to build up the desire to reach it so that you give as much effort as possible to get there. Having a strong will to reach your objectives will boost your chances to break through and realize mental victory which will make real victory possible.

Motivational visualizations can be used for different purposes in your personal life, which can improve your overall performance in your athletic life as well especially if you are trying to give up a vice like smoking, alcohol, uncontrollable anger or fear, over eating, partying, gambling, etc.

CHAPTER 9: VISUALIZATION TECHNIQUES: PROBLEM SOLVING VISUALIZATIONS

Visualizations should be done properly and directed towards the best problem solving techniques. For this reason determining what will work best is the most important step. For this reason we are going to look at how most athletes approach their problems.

How do most athletes approach problem solving?

There are many ways athletes approach their problems and attempt to solve them. "Attempt" is the key word.

These are the most often seen examples of how athletes approach problem solving:

The anger solution

They get mad at their problems and get frustrated to the point where their brain helps little or nothing because they're so overcome by their negative emotions.

Anger is an emotional reaction that is normal and common but not necessarily a solution that will bring about positive results. When attempting to solve your problems, emotions need to be set aside so that you can better concentrate on the real problem that needs to be addressed.

Managing anger is difficult for some and can take time to overcome but specific activities such as visualizations, meditation, and yoga are a great way to start.

The "blame-game" solution

Athletes who blame others for their mistakes or problems knowingly make an effort not to blame themselves. Blaming others for your errors or problems is the easy way out of justifying lack of success but does not solve the problem at all.

Others blame their equipment and/or surroundings without considering that changes in climate and surroundings will affect all competitors and not just them. Blaming equipment failure is simply not what should be focused on since proper preparation can easily solve this problem. Sometimes the equipment might not have any flaws at all and is just a way of blaming something other than themselves. Taking responsibility for their actions is the hardest but the most productive way to advance to a real solution.

The "whining" solution

Whining and complaining makes your voice be heard by others and yourself but only delays the inevitable result of failure since steps are not being taken to remedy the situation. Whining starts at a young age when you don't get what you want but the worst thing that can happen is being given that which you're complaining for because it does not allow you to solve the problem correctly.

Learning to cope with a negative performance should be a key element when developing mental toughness. Becoming mentally tough does not happen because you have had an easy path to success. Its normally comes from not giving in to negative results and failure.

The "stop-trying" solution

Not making any effort to succeed and basically giving up is a choice some athletes make but it's not one to be proud of since so many better options exist. Training your brain to find alternatives to succeed instead of giving up will always be a better path and a more fruitful one.

The "repeat-offender" solution

The repeat-offender is the athlete that keeps making the same mistake over and over expecting a different result. We have all been victims of this mental error but it can become a turning point for those of you who acknowledge this fault and want to make a true change in your results.

Simply changing how you solve your problem is already an improvement even though it's not a precise direction which you're following but it's a different path and a different path will give you a chance to change things.

The "trial and error" solution

The "trial and error" solution is simply trying new approaches to your problem and seeing if they are a solution to the problem. The outcome will be that you will eventually find the right solution to your problem but it might take you long than you would like or longer than you can afford.

This is a much better approach than the last mentioned solutions but you can learn to make even better choices by separating certain factors and conditions from your options and that's what we will see next.

The "best probability" solution

When solving problems, we all know that we have alternatives and choices we can make to find a solution but knowing which one of them will be more useful and worth visualizing on is what matters the most.

Using probabilities helps you quantify that which you are trying to solve in your mind.

For example, if you find that every time you warm up you start to get nervous but don't know why. Eventually, once you complete your warm up nerves go away and you feel fine. Now you know that focusing on visualizing on your actual performance would only account for less than

10% of the problem since you know that the warm up is really 90% of your problem. You can work on your performance mentally but finding a solving to your warm up problem will provide you with the most valuable results since it accounts for 90% of your problem and will result in a 90% improvement in your overall performance.

Another example would be if you find that every time you are in a pressure situation you freeze and underperform. That key moment accounts for 100% of your results based on past performances. Since it will represent the most change in what you want to achieve you should focus 100% of your visualization sessions on finding solutions to that key moment. That way you will be most productive with your time.

Focusing on what matters the most will make the biggest change so learn to concentrate and direct your visualizations on what will help you the most and not on unimportant problems that even if solved won't create a true improvement in your results.

CHAPTER 10: VISUALIZATION TECHNIQUES: GOAL ORIENTED VISUALIZATIONS

Performance based goals vs results based goals

Before starting any goal oriented visualizations you should have a clear image of what you want to gain from visualizing and what the best path will be to get there.

What are performance based goals?

Performance based goals are simple goals that can be reached by doing things you know you need to do to be successful. These can be physical or mental. Not looking at the competition or family and friends while performing is a great example of a performance based goal you can have for yourself. If are able to reach that goal after competing then you have accomplished what you set out to do and will be much closer to reaching your results based goals.

Another example of a performance based goal is to focus on staying calm and breathe during competition. Reaching this goal at the end will be your objective. Achieving this goal will help you get much closer to being successful and realizing your potential. It's a simple and easy to obtain goal that you have 100% control over. If you don't make it the first time, you know that if you keep trying you will eventually get there and can then create a new harder or different performance based goal.

These are other examples of performance goals that athletes can have:

- Do 1 more push-up every day.
- Stretch for 10 minutes a day.
- Breathe in and out under pressure.
- Focus your eyes on the task at hand and not on your surroundings.
- Stay calm when underperforming.
- Stay energized when you feel yourself freezing under difficult situations.

You can create your own performance based goals and make them harder want as long as their attainable.

What are results based goals?

Results based goals are goals you make for yourself which are focused on end results and not the process to get there. Some examples of a results based goal is to win, to reach the final of a competition, to lift "x" weight, to have the best time, to finish first, etc. Athletes can have different goals and still reach the same objective.

Some examples of results based goals that athletes can have are:

- Win 5 championships before the end of the year.
- Break a world record.
- Finish first in your country.
- Win your first medal or trophy.
- Help your team get to their first final.
- Jump higher than you have ever before.
- Run your fastest time.
- Swim the furthest you ever have.
- Reach the finish line before everyone else.

Results based goals are the result of consistent, organized, and gradually increasing performance goals.

When visualizing you need to visualize success in both reaching your performance and results based goals. You can alternate days to focus on one and then the other or simply stick to performance based goals first and once you feel that you are comfortably reaching them, you can move on to results based goals.

Having goals is the key to moving forward and should be visualized on at least once a week so that you have a clear image of what you are working on to reach. It's the best way to move forward and see yourself advance through the process. Without goals you won't have a path to follow towards success. Map out that path in your mind through your visualizations and then turn them into reality by putting them into practice when training or competing.

CHAPTER 11: THE VISUALIZATION PROCESS FOR MAXIMUM SWIMMING RESULTS

When you visualize and want to achieve maximum results you will need to follow these exact steps every time. If you change or eliminate any step, you will end up changing the outcome of the visualization session.

These steps are:

1st: Find a quiet place where you won't be disturbed.

2nd: Place a mat, towel, blanket, or chair where you are planning to visualize.

3rd: Make sure you had your shake or a light meal about a half hour before visualizing.

4th: Choose a position in which you will be comfortable in for the entire session. This could be: sitting on a chair, lying down on a mat, sitting in a position on the floor, kneeling on a mat, or any other comfortable visualization position mentioned before.

5th: Begin your breathing pattern. If you want to calm and relax yourself you should choose to breathe more air out than you do air in. For example, breathe in 4 seconds and then breathe out for 6 seconds. When trying to energize yourself because you feel too relaxed or just woke up, you would breathe more air in than out in a specific ratio which you can decide beforehand. For example, breathe 5 seconds in and 3 seconds out. Remember each sequence of breathing needs to be repeated at least 4 to 6 times to allow your breathing to slow the mind down and get you in a state of calmness to best visualize. For all breathing patterns you will breathe in through your nose and out through your mouth.

6th: Once you are done completing your breathing patterns in the manner explained in the breathing patterns chapter, you should begin to focus on something you want to obtain, achieve, or simply preview in your mind. Choose what type of visualization session you want to have. You can focus on your goals, on motivating yourself, or on solving a problem you have.

7th: This thought should now evolve to a short or long mental movie clip you are creating in your mind to help you achieve what you want in your mind first, with the goal to eventually make it happen in a real life situation. Be as specific as possible and stay relaxed in the process. This seventh step adds visualizing to the process.

8th: Athletes need to use breathing to finish their visualization sessions to end as they began. If you don't have to compete on the same day, you can use slow breathing patterns such as the example below:

Normal slow breathing pattern: Start by taking air in through your nose slowly and counting to 5. Then, release slowly counting back down from 5 to 1. You should repeat this process 4 to 10 times until you feel completely relaxed and ready to visualize. Athletes should focus on breathing in through the nose and out through the mouth for this type of breathing pattern.

If you have to compete the same day you should energize your mind and body at the end by using fast breathing patterns such as the one below:

Normal fast breathing pattern: Start by taking air in through your nose slowly and counting to 5. Then, release slowly counting back down from 3 to 1. You should repeat this process 6 to 10 times until you feel completely relaxed but energized. Athletes should focus on breathing in through the nose and out through the mouth for this type of breathing pattern.

CHAPTER 12: SWIMMING MOTIVATIONAL VISUALIZATION SESSION

To begin your session:

To begin your session have in mind what will be the main topic for your visualization session. In this case we will start with a goal you have never been able to accomplish such as reaching the top of a mountain, or finishing a run before a specific time, or reaching your highest vertical jump, or swimming a minimum of 50 laps without a break. Visualizations should be used to improve your training sessions as well as when you are in live competitions.

Time and day: Saturday morning, an hour before physically starting your training routine. (Preparing a training calendar to plan your sessions will help you to be more consistent and will motivate you to repeat sessions as often as possible).

Location: Laying down on a yoga mat in a dark room at home.

Equipment: towel, water, comfortable clothes, and a yoga mat.

Preparation: Before starting this session I had a mango and strawberry milkshake with low fat yogurt. Besides having this shake I did some static stretching to get myself in the right state of mind and worked on focusing on my breathing.

Visualization session begins (I will use an example just as I would be visualizing. Even though I will be using the word "I" often, it's necessary to help you understand what I am feeling and trying to accomplish with this routine):

I begin my 3-6 breathing pattern by breathing in for 3 seconds through my nose and releasing the air through my mouth slowly for 6 seconds. I repeat this 4 times to make sure my heart rate has slowed done and I am relaxed.

While laying down I begin wiggling my toes since I am barefoot and then move on to my calves as I focus on them and to make them release all tension. After that I continue to my thighs and gluts, looking to make them relax any tension that has accumulated.

I keep breathing slow and deep breaths in the same pattern as I begin to see my intensity level slow down so that I can control my thoughts and emotions better.

I now focus on my stomach and try to integrate my breathing with my abdominal muscles by inflating my belly as I breathe in and deflating it as I breathe out. After that I move on to expanding my lungs as I breathe in and contracting them as I breathe out.

I wiggle my finger tips to allow them to gently open my hand and accept the moment. My arms and shoulders begin to relax towards the floor and ease flat on the ground.

Now, I move on to my neck and lower head muscles that are working to keep my head straight. I let them give in to gravity as I tilt slightly to one side thus allowing my head to be in a comfortable position.

To get in the right mindset I begin to imagine a scenic view that I think is memorable and causes me to feel inspired.

I am at the top of a mountain that has a view so broad that you can see the entire city from there. The breeze is strong and cool. My hair is moving everywhere but is so refreshing that I simply absorb the moment. The ground is cold but firm. The feeling is liberating and inspiring. I can see cars and people moving far beneath me. The view is outstanding as I walk slowly on the top of the mountain.

Now it's time to start with the visualization session.

I begin my visualization session by calculating the pace at which I need to run to finish before a specific time. I stretch my legs and jump around to get them warmed up. They feel ready to push to the limit and all my emotions want that to happen. I get my stop watch ready and click the button to start. My legs begin to push hard off the ground. I know my body needs to lean forward to get myself in the right position to maintain the pace I need. I am turning my arms quickly and efficiently trying to coordinate each step I take. As I start to feel tired I know I need to take longer strides and so I start reaching further and further outwards with my legs.

I take a moment to focus on my breathing pattern as I now breathe in for 3 seconds and release for 3 seconds to maintain the intensity of the run.

Its feels great and I feel completely energized. I check my watch and see that I am a few seconds behind my ideal time so I start to run faster. As I get near the finish line I begin to sprint to guarantee myself the time I want to see on my stop watch.

I take another moment to focus on my breathing pattern as I now breathe in for 2 seconds and release for 2 seconds to maintain the intensity of the run.

I am about to finish and feel my legs are hurting and tired but I'm too close so I don't stop. I lean in at the end and finish with a record time. I knew that I could do it if I put all my effort to making it happen.

What a feeling it is to reach a goal that has been so difficult for me to reach and how long it's taken but all those tries were worth this last run.

To finish my visualization session I try to control my breathing pattern by breathing in 6 seconds and breathing out for 4 seconds. This will slow my heart rate and help me control my emotions and thoughts. I repeat this breathing pattern three times.

To restart my body I begin to wiggle my toes again but now with the purpose of awakening my senses. I move on to my calves and upper legs moving them gently from side to side. I breathe again through my stomach bringing air in and expanding my stomach and then breathing out and bringing my stomach inwards. After that, I move on to expand and contract my lungs while I focus on my breathing pattern. My fingers wiggle gently to wake up my extremities. My forearms and shoulders start to regain strength. My head begins to turn back to the center as I slowly start to sit up on the yoga mat. I now stand up and am done with my visualization session.

Finishing up: When you finish you should pick up your equipment and write down anything you felt was relevant to the training session and anything you think will be useful as a reminder before or during competition. It can be as simply as how you walked or how you looked so that you can dress and look the same way you did when you visualized to get as close to looking like you did when you were successful in your visualizations. Plan your next session and decide if you want to repeat the same mental images or want to move on to another moment in your mind that you believe will benefit you or that needs some work.

CHAPTER 13: SWIMMING PROBLEM SOLVING VISUALIZATION SESSION

To begin your session:

To begin your session decide what problem you are planning on solving or fixing. We are going to focus on overcoming nerves in key moments of my competition and to overcome any fear and anxiousness at the same time.

Time and day: Wednesday morning, three days before my competition. (Preparing a training calendar to plan your sessions will help you to be more consistent and will motivate you to repeat sessions as often as possible).

Location: Laying down on a blanket in a dark room.

Equipment: towel, water, comfortable clothes, and a blanket.

Preparation: Before starting this session I had a coconut, pineapple, banana milkshake with some milk protein added. Besides having this shake I did some static stretching to get myself in the right state of mind and worked on focusing on my breathing.

Visualization session begins:

I begin my 3-6 breathing pattern by breathing in for 3 seconds through my nose and releasing the air through my mouth slowly for 6 seconds. I repeat this 4 times to make sure my heart rate has slowed done and I am relaxed.

While laying down I begin wiggling my toes since I am barefoot and then move on to my calves as I focus on them and to make them release all tension. After that I continue to my thighs and gluts, looking to make them relax any tension that has accumulated.

I keep breathing slow and deep breaths in the same pattern as I begin to see my intensity level slow down so that I can control my thoughts and emotions better.

I now focus on my stomach and try to integrate my breathing with my abdominal muscles by inflating my belly as I breathe in and deflating it as I breathe out. After that I move on to expanding my lungs as I breathe in and contracting them as I breathe out.

I wiggle my finger tips to allow them to gently open my hand and accept the moment. My arms and shoulders begin to relax towards the floor and ease flat on the ground.

Now, I move on to my neck and lower head muscles that are working to keep my head straight. I let them give in to gravity as I tilt slightly to one side thus allowing my head to be in a comfortable position.

In order to relax my mind and thoughts I try to imagine a great place that fills me with humbleness and gratitude. I am at the bottom of a waterfall that seems calm but at the same time very powerful. The intensity with which the water lands is overwhelming and loud. Even though it's loud it makes me feel calm and relaxed. I just sit and listen to the water coming down. The trees and plants surrounding me are vivid green and marvelous. I walk into the water and go near the waterfall. It's warm and soothing. As some water splashes over my face I find nature to be part of my life in an important way.

Even though I prefer not to leave this moment, it's time to advance to my visualization session.

Now I begin my visualization session.

I am about to perform but feel very nervous. I don't know why but I do and want it to go away. I look around to see if others seem to be nervous or on the edge of a break down but I see everyone is focused and warming up. There's no clue I can see in their body language that tells me they are nervous. I know I am afraid to lose and just want to get it over with but I suddenly realize that enjoying the moment will make things easier so I stretch a smile on my face and concentrate on my breathing since I notice I am also holding my breath.

I take a moment to focus on my breathing pattern and breathe in for 8 seconds and release for 4 seconds.

It's helping me to calm down so I repeat this breathing pattern five more times.

I want to win and know that if I don't start to overcome my fears and learn to concentrate my energy on my goals this won't happen. Now that I feel more relaxed, I am ready and begin to feel more confident. Now is the time to act. I push myself to the end and surpass my target. Victory is finally mine.

My approach towards fear and nervousness has helped me to overcome the hardest of adversities. Knowing yourself is half the battle. The other half is in learning how to unlock the limits we set for ourselves.

To finish my visualization session I try to control my breathing pattern by breathing in 6 seconds and breathing out for 4 seconds. This will slow my heart rate and help me control my emotions and thoughts. I repeat this breathing pattern three times.

To restart my body I begin to wiggle my toes again but now with the purpose of awakening my senses. I move on to my calves and upper legs moving them gently from side to side. I breathe again through my stomach bringing air in and expanding my stomach and then breathing out and bringing my stomach inwards. After that, I move on to expand and contract my lungs while I focus on my breathing pattern. My fingers wiggle gently to wake up my extremities. My forearms and shoulders start to regain strength. My head begins to turn back to the center as I slowly start to sit up on the blanket. I now stand up and am done with my visualization session.

Finishing up: When you finish you should pick up your equipment and write down anything you felt was relevant to the training session and anything you think will be useful as a reminder before or during competition. It can be as simply as how you walked or how you looked so that you can dress and look the same way you did when you visualized to get as close to looking like you did when you were successful in your visualizations.

Plan your next session and decide if you want to repeat the same mental images or want to move on to another moment in your mind that you believe will benefit you or that needs some work.

CHAPTER 14: SWIMMING GOAL ORIENTED VISUALIZATION SESSION

To begin your session:

To begin your session decide what results based goal you will be visualizing on. In this case we will start with seeing yourself winning the competition and lifting the trophy or receiving the medal.

Results based goal: to visualize myself being confident as I win the competition.

Time and day: Friday night, the day before my competition. (Preparing a training calendar to plan your sessions will help you to be more consistent and will motivate you to repeat sessions as often as possible).

Location: Laying down on a towel in a dark room.

Equipment: towel, water, comfortable clothes, and a fan (to stay cool and have a sound that will help me stay relaxed but focused). Using a fan is an option and is particular to what I like but you can choose something else like classical music.

Preparation: Before starting this session I had a banana, strawberry, and coconut milk shake. Besides having this shake I did some yoga to get myself in the right state of mind and worked on focusing on my breathing.

Visualization session begins:

I begin my 3-6 breathing pattern by breathing in for 3 seconds through my nose and releasing the air through my mouth slowly for 6 seconds. I repeat this 4 times to make sure my heart rate has slowed done and I am relaxed.

While laying down I begin wiggling my toes since I am barefoot and then move on to my calves as I focus on them and to make them release all tension. After that I continue to my thighs and gluts, looking to make them relax any tension that has accumulated.

I keep breathing slow and deep breaths in the same pattern as I begin to see my intensity level slow down so that I can control my thoughts and emotions better.

I now focus on my stomach and try to integrate my breathing with my abdominal muscles by inflating my belly as I breathe in and deflating it as I breathe out. After that I move on to expanding my lungs as I breathe in and contracting them as I breathe out.

I wiggle my finger tips to allow them to gently open my hand and accept the moment. My arms and shoulders begin to relax towards the floor and ease flat on the ground.

Now, I move on to my neck and lower head muscles that are working to keep my head straight. I let them give in to gravity as I tilt slightly to one side thus allowing my head to be in a comfortable position.

To get in the right mindset I begin to imagine a view that I think is memorable and gets me in a great mood. I am at the beach and it's dark so I am able to see the moon and stars. I can see and hear waves splashing into each other and how the water sways back and forth. My feet can feel the warm water and I can see the sand run through my fingers. The wind is blowing gently across my body. The temperature is just right. A bit warm but not too humid.

Its feels like a moment you never want to leave. That's when you know you're ready to start with your visualization session.

As I begin to visualize, I see myself with a smile on my face even though I feel tired and sweaty. The competition sees me and acknowledges my success but the true feeling of personal satisfaction is being felt close to my heart as it continues to pound hard. My legs feel tight but I just shake that tightness off and walk around. My friends and family congratulate me on my success and are very proud of me. I feel extremely excited and inspired by what I just accomplished.

I take a moment to focus on my breathing pattern as I now breathe in for 4 seconds and release for 4 seconds.

They call my name and my heart stops. I know I've earned it and want to run up to receive my reward but walk slowly to enjoy the moment. My clothes are still a little humid from the competition and I'm still sweating. My posture looks strong and straight as I am proud of who I have become and what I have accomplished. My walk is confident and energetic. My hands sway in a rhythmic manner and my head is held up high. As I am awarded the prize I thank everyone for having allowed me to be a part of a great competition. As I walk away I show my friends and family my award and smile.

I have achieved my goal and have accomplished what I set out to do by being disciplined, hard-working, and positive with my training and my attitude.

To finish my visualization session I try to control my breathing pattern by breathing in 6 seconds and breathing out for 4 seconds. This will slow my heart rate and help me control my emotions and thoughts. I repeat this breathing pattern three times.

To restart my body I begin to wiggle my toes again but now with the purpose of awakening my senses. I move on to my calves and upper legs moving them gently from side to side. I breathe again through my stomach bringing air in and expanding my stomach and then breathing out and bringing my stomach inwards. After that, I move on to expand and contract my lungs while I focus on my breathing pattern. My fingers wiggle gently to wake up my extremities. My forearms and shoulders start to regain strength. My head begins to turn back to the center as I slowly start to sit up on my towel. I now stand up and am done with my visualization session.

Finishing up: When you finish you should pick up your equipment and write down anything you felt was relevant to the training session and anything you think will be useful as a reminder before or during competition. It can be as simply as how you walked or how you looked so that you can dress and look the same way you did when you visualized to get as close to looking like you did when you were successful in your visualizations. Plan your next session and decide if you want to repeat the same mental images or want to move on to another moment in your mind that you believe will benefit you or that needs some work.

To begin your performance based goal session:

To begin your session decide what performance based goal you will be reaching and surpassing which can be as easy or hard as you want and as broad or simple as you would like.

Performance based goal: to visualize myself being energetic and moving my feet.

Time and day: Monday afternoon, three days before competing. (Preparing a training calendar to plan your sessions will help you to be more consistent and will motivate you to repeat sessions as often as possible).

Location: Laying down on a towel in a dark room.

Equipment: towel, water, comfortable clothes, and some nature music of rain falling slowly in the background.

Preparation: Before starting this session I had a lean protein lunch did some yoga to get myself in the right state of mind and worked my breathing patterns.

Visualization session begins:

I begin my 3-6 breathing pattern by breathing in for 3 seconds through my nose and releasing the air through my mouth slowly for 6 seconds. I repeat this 4 times to make sure my heart rate has slowed done and I am relaxed.

While laying down I begin wiggling my toes since I am barefoot and then move on to my calves as I focus on them and to make them release all tension. After that I continue to my thighs and gluts, looking to make them relax any tension that has accumulated.

I keep breathing slow and deep breaths in the same pattern as I begin to see my intensity level slow down so that I can control my thoughts and emotions better.

I now focus on my stomach and try to integrate my breathing with my abdominal muscles by inflating my belly as I breathe in and deflating it as I breathe out. After that I move on to expanding my lungs as I breathe in and contracting them as I breathe out.

I wiggle my finger tips to allow them to gently open my hand and accept the moment. My arms and shoulders begin to relax towards the floor and ease flat on the ground.

Now, I move on to my neck and lower head muscles that are working to keep my head straight. I let them give in to gravity as I tilt slightly to one side thus allowing my head to be in a comfortable position.

To prepare my mind and body I close my eyes and imagine a place that I know will calm my senses and get me in the right mood to visualize.

The sun is starting to come up and I am in a large field of grass as far as I can see. Its feels like I am in the middle of farm land. It's all green, no cement buildings, no cars, no noise, no cell phones, and no people. Birds are flying around and the ground is moist. I walk through the grass and see some trees on the right that are tall and move with the wind. The air is cool and dry. I lift my head to receive the sun as it rises from the ground and begins to shine bright on the world. I raise my arms and enjoy the smell of a new day and a new opportunity to be alive.

Now I am ready to begin my visualization session.

My visualization session starts with noise in the background and many distractions around me but I don't look around. I relax myself by focusing on my breathing.

I take a moment to focus on my breathing pattern as I now breathe in for 3 seconds and release for 3 seconds. I repeat this process 3 times.

As I start, I turn my face to show a strong and decisive mood. My attitude is directed towards reaching my goal no matter what. I move my feet around and feel the energy in body start to flow. I know that I perform my best when my energy levels are high and I am in constant movement so I'm ready for action. My reflexes are sharp and ready to go. I am accomplishing what I set out to do as I am staying in motion by moving my feet and feeling energetic by targeting my emotions on a strong and confident attitude.

I am done. I have fulfilled my goal to perform specific performance tasks that will get me to my ultimate goal which is to be successful but that will only happen if I reach my performance goals first.

To finish my visualization session I try to control my breathing pattern by breathing in 6 seconds and breathing out for 4 seconds. This will slow my heart rate and help me control my emotions and thoughts. I repeat this breathing pattern three times.

To restart my body I begin to wiggle my toes again but now with the purpose of awakening my senses. I move on to my calves and upper legs moving them gently from side to side. I breathe again through my stomach bringing air in and expanding my stomach and then breathing out and bringing my stomach inwards. After that, I move on to expand and contract my lungs while I focus on my breathing pattern. My fingers wiggle gently to wake up my extremities. My forearms and shoulders start to regain strength. My head begins to turn back to the center as I slowly start to sit up on my towel. I now stand up and am done with my visualization session.

Finishing up: When you finish you should pick up your equipment and write down anything you felt was relevant to the training session and anything you think will be useful as a reminder before or during competition. It can be as simply as how you walked or how you looked so that you can dress and look the same way you did when you visualized to get as close to looking like you did when you were successful in your visualizations.

Plan your next session and decide if you want to repeat the same mental images or want to move on to another moment in your mind that you believe will benefit you or that needs some work.

CLOSING THOUGHTS

Visualizing will make a significant change in your performance no matter what you think your limitations are. The mind has no limits and can allow you to achieve that which you think is impossible. You will learn to develop your visualizing abilities with some practice and will find you can have a lot of fun and joy by imagining what is truly possible for you when you believe you can make a change. Remember that visualizing what you want to happen in your mind will show you the path to ultimate success in real life.

OTHER GREAT TITLES BY THIS AUTHOR

Becoming Mentally Tougher In

SWIMMING

by Using Meditation

Reaching Your Potential by Controlling
Your Inner Thoughts

By
JOSEPH CORREA
Certified Meditation Instructor

Made in the USA
Lexington, KY
19 August 2016